Soar to Your Destiny

5 winning success strategies

Dr. Amanda H. Goodson

Soar to Your Destiny
by Dr. Amanda H. Goodson

Fourth edition
© 2020 by Amanda H. Goodson
All rights reserved.

Edited by Adam Colwell's WriteWorks, LLC: Adam Colwell and Ginger Colwell
Cover Design by Kimb Manson
Typesetting by Inktobook.com
Published by Amanda Goodson

Printed in the United States of America
ISBN-13:9780615798394
ISBN-10:061579839X

Bible verses quoted are taken from the THE HOLY BIBLE, NEW INTERNATIONAL VERSION (NIV)®. Copyright © 1973, 1978, 1984, 2011 by Biblica, Inc.™. Used by permission of Zondervan.

www.ingramcontent.com/pod-product-compliance
Lightning Source LLC
Chambersburg PA
CBHW032018190326
41520CB00007B/525

Dedication

———

To every person who is seeking to be great in life.
Never give out, never give in, and never give up!
To my family and friends who are always so supportive of my pursuits.
To Rosalyn. Thank you for all you do.

Table of Contents

Believe in the *Possible*

––––––

Y ou are purposed to be great. Greatness begins by developing a mindset that molds your character. The success you will experience depends on the mental image you hold onto in your mind. Your brain thinks in pictures. It creates visuals of what you perceive or believe, so you need to come up with pictures that have positive outcomes. Mental images are indicators of your vision, self-image, and self-esteem.

You want to live a *great* life. Question is, are you willing to soar to higher heights to reach your potential on a regular basis? To "soar" is to place yourself in a dimension of tranquil assurance where you not only launch but remain airborne, capable of staying in that elevated space for as long as you desire to reach your peak.

Although you possess the ability to soar, you might doubt this possibility for yourself. It's hard for you to see how you can accomplish far above what is expected of you or far beyond your circumstances. Perhaps it's because of uncertainty, fear, or even untruths that people have told about you that you have processed as truth.

The last time you looked in the mirror, what did you see? *Who* did you see? Was it the person whose mindset is tainted with self-doubt, or was it the real you, the person capable of achieving greatness?

I believe you are a winner and always have been. In fact, I believe it so strongly that I want you to trust this truth for yourself. In *Soar to Your Destiny*, I will unveil five success strategies that will cause you to see and believe that you are a victor.

A champion.

A conqueror from the inside out.

I will stress the importance of using the power and potential already in existence within you to do great things. You have so much promise inside of you. It just needs to be stirred up, raised up, and unleashed. It is waiting to emerge. It may be that you require more focus, direction, education, skills, or maturity in specific areas—but I believe, once you have completed *Soar to Your Destiny*, that you will be ready and able to walk in the authority destined for you. After all, all things are possible when you believe in yourself and in the source of your authority (Matthew 19:26).

You possess the capacity and competence to make things happen in a way that will transform who you are, what you do, and the people you touch in an awesome way, but living in that power requires you to think like a winner so that you can see the way toward your purpose. *Soar to Your Destiny* will equip you with the attitude to rise above everything around you while still having your feet planted on a stable foundation. It's like living in two places at once. Even though you're firmly rooted, your thoughts are not limited to where you are.

Join me! Together, let's empower you to soar, see yourself in your higher state—and believe in the possible!

Success Strategy #1

You Are Meant to Soar

Your very DNA is mapped so you can soar.

I once led a class where I asked each of my students about his or her experience with flying in an airplane. We started with the fact that an airplane flies high above the ground at hundreds of miles per hour to reach its destination. We talked about how an aircraft experiences four forces to get off the ground:

1. **Drag:** the force opposing the plane when in motion.
2. **Weight:** the force that seeks to keep the plane on the ground.
3. **Speed:** the ability to move forward at a velocity that causes the plane to get off the ground.
4. **Lift:** the force that creates differential pressure on the wings that causes the airplane to rise above the ground and fly.

Then I had the students apply these four forces to their lives. We thought of speed and lift as representing positive personal experiences, while drag and weight were indicative of personal experiences that were not so positive. The students smiled as they considered speed and lift, but thoughts about drag and weight caused them to be sad and even anxious.

Some of the answers they gave of negative experiences included the following:

- worry
- complaining
- stress
- anger
- frustration
- being overwhelmed
- being overworked
- loneliness
- laziness
- negativity
- bullies
- backstabbers
- untrustworthy people
- impatience

However, the speed and lift list featured a variety of upbeat responses:

- laughter
- happiness
- life
- faithfulness
- gratefulness
- fun tasks
- shopping
- singing
- dancing
- friends
- hope
- health

Speed and lift refer to the pleasant realities of life, while drag and weight represent the difficulties.

SOARING IS MORE THAN FLYING

If we are to eventually fly, we have to deal with our share of both positive and negative personal experiences. We must focus on more than mere flying. An airplane doesn't fly the same way birds do. They soar. Birds ride the drafts to sail or hover in the air, often at great heights that belie their size and weight. When we have the opportunity to witness an eagle or a hawk soaring high in the sky, it is awe-inspiring. I live in Arizona, home of the Grand Canyon. One of the world's natural wonders, the canyon is home to several California Condors that can be seen from spring through early fall. They are the largest flying birds in North America and can soar up to 15,000 feet in elevation.

It takes a lot of energy to reach that altitude, but once there, condors use the surrounding air currents to maintain their height. They rarely have to flap their wings. Similarly, an airplane uses more fuel during takeoff than it does at its soaring altitude. If we can do what it takes to face our challenges, get off the ground, and fly up to our soaring altitude, staying there will use less of our energy—but provide a vast, panoramic view of our situation that will give us needed perspective.

I now realize that I can soar, but for much of my life, I was content to stay on the ground. As a high school student, I took part in a math competition and won eighth place in the entire school, the only girl and African American in the top ten. Yet I was shocked when my name was called because I never viewed myself as being smart. Everyone told me I was average, especially my teachers, and that seeped away my confidence. I never actively sought to be the best I could be. I did try hard in math, and I played clarinet in the marching band, bass clarinet in the concert band, and piano in the jazz band. Yet even there, whenever the jazz director pointed over to me to do an improvisational solo during a song, I couldn't do it. I didn't have the confidence to try.

I definitely wasn't getting off the ground. I was told I wouldn't be successful in life because my grades were average, and I operated in that assumption. Yet the weight of that expectation, and the nagging self-doubt it created, kept me down.

As my senior year neared an end, I realized I needed to decide what I was going to do as an adult. With my father's encouragement, I went to the library to research what professions paid well that might fit with my two interests, math and music. It was clear. Engineers and accountants generally made money while musicians didn't. So, I thought, *I'll take engineering*. I then made an appointment with a high school counselor.

"Girls are not engineers," I was told, point blank. "Maybe you should go into the military or be a nurse."

That was my first experience with gender bias—and I didn't listen to it. It wasn't that I thought there was anything wrong with being a nurse or in the military. It's just I knew those weren't the paths for me.

So, despite my counselor's advice to not go to a traditional four-year college, I decided I would, starting with Preface, a summer pre-engineering program for high school graduates at Tuskegee University, the school my dad had attended. It was there where my instructors first told me that I was smart. That inspired me to apply myself and study like I never had before. I got results, too, along with more encouragement from my professors. They lifted me to new heights.

Then, from that lofty vantage point, I looked around and saw other students who were doing what I had been doing earlier, and thought to myself, *Wow. This is what 'average' looks like*. From that moment on, I decided I was not going to be average and decided to soar as a young engineering student at Tuskegee—a decision that ultimately landed me with my first post-graduation job at NASA.

I made a choice to not allow my circumstances, grades, or other people to cause drag and weight that would define me and keep me grounded. I discovered that I could do whatever I set my mind to do.

Several years after I started working at NASA, I went back to my middle school to talk to the students. The principal had been my history teacher back when I was a student there.

Someone asked him, "Did you ever think Amanda would grow up to do something like this?"

He answered honestly that he hadn't.

My teachers expected me to be average. They told me that I was average, and they assumed I would continue to be so.

Before Wilbur and Orville Wright showed us that we could actually take to the air, most people expected that humans could never rise above the ground. My teachers didn't think that I could rise above where I was. But just like those in Kitty Hawk, North Carolina who saw the Wright Brother's first airplane take flight, once they saw that I could soar, they thought it was pretty cool.

So did I.

WHAT'S *REALLY* SAFE?

I have a friend who never flew in an airplane until she was 18 years old. She was afraid of the possibility of falling to her death from thousands of feet in the air, so she kept to the roads whenever she needed to leave town. However, when it was time for her to go to college far from home, flying was the only option that made sense.

She had grown up watching presidents on TV walk up to Air Force One, ascend an outdoor staircase, and wave before entering the plane. So, as she counted down to her first-ever flight, she imagined walking through the brisk air from the terminal gate to her aircraft.

She imagined her heart pounding with each step up the stairs before proceeding into the dark, narrow confines of the fuselage.

To her surprise, there was no walk outside and no staircase to climb when she boarded the plane. All she had to do was stride through an enclosed jet bridge that extended from the airport terminal to the aircraft. Once she was inside the plane, the seats and center aisle comfortably reminded her of bus trips she had taken with her family as a kid. She felt a few flutters as the plane sped down the runway for takeoff, but after that, she settled in for the smooth flight. In what seemed like no time at all, she was at her destination.

A trip that would've taken her all day to drive took less than two hours on the airplane. She couldn't help but think about how much time she had wasted in the past because of her fear of flying. From then on, she flew as often as she could.

My friend had always viewed flying on an airplane as something only for those willing to take risks, not her. But once she soared above her fears (figuratively and literally), she began racking up the frequent flyer miles. Truth is, the website www.planecrashinfo.com reports that the odds of being killed on an airplane are one in 4.7 *million* across 78 major international airlines. The odds in the United States indicate an even more favorable safety record. Conversely, the World Health Organization and World Bank estimate that there are 1.4 deaths per year in the United States for every 10,000 cars on the road. Not only was my friend wasting time driving from place to place, she was taking far more risk with her well-being.

Sometimes, we think we are being safe when we really aren't. We have to be willing to take bold steps if we want to have bold experiences. When I spoke at a women's leadership conference in 2019, I met a woman named Meg. She had spent her childhood learning how to be a wife and mother—and nothing else. From a young age, she was taught those were her roles. They defined her place in life, and informed what her destiny would be. Even though Meg had a passionate love and talent for art and storytelling, her parents' mantra was, "Make sure you marry someone who can support you if those are the things you want to pursue." Her mother told Meg that being a nurturing parent and having a successful career were incompatible goals, and that she would never be truly fulfilled as a businessperson alone.

Today, Meg is a published author and owns a successful editing business. She didn't play it safe according to her parent's expectations. Instead she buckled down, boldly pursued her dreams, and is reaping incredible rewards. Even more, Meg's journey inspired her mother to revisit her aspirations: she went to college and is finishing her degree in psychology at the age of 47.

A DIFFERENT LIFE

My life would've been totally different had I allowed the drag and weight of mediocrity to keep me on the ground. I would never have been exposed to the international team NASA employed for space exploration, or to the vast knowledge they possessed. I would never have traveled to the incredible places I have visited as part of my work. My income certainly would've been lower, the quality of my family life would've been different, and my impact on my community would've been far less.

Since I realized I didn't want to be average, I've worked daily to soar. I know drag and weight will come at some point. It may be a difficult technical challenge at work that seems insurmountable. It could be a person who doubts in my ability. Whatever it is, I understand that if I move forward (speed) and apply enough force (lift), I can soar.

What about you? Compile your own lists of positive and negative experiences that fit where you are right now. What operates as a drag or weight, keeping you from living the different life that you want? What gives you speed and lift, empowering you to rise above your circumstances and providing the boost you need to do great things?

When you hear the negative people around you, decide that you won't let them keep you from soaring. Angie grew up in a small town in the south. A smart young lady, she unfortunately had negativity all around her, and endured some tough times with her family and in her community. It was so bad, she quit high school. It was not that Angie was a failure and couldn't finish her education, but everyone and everything around her told her she couldn't. Eventually, knowing she needed to make a better life for herself, Angie decided to go get her GED, her first attempt to soar. Even then, others said she couldn't do better, so Angie went to junior college—and then to a four-year college where she got an engineering degree. Upon graduation, she was hired by a major organization as an engineer.

Angie soared and maintained her elevation, going from a high school dropout no one believed in to an engineer who is now a senior leader at her company. She decided she had more in her to give and she pursued it.

You can, too. If you need to make time for yourself to plan the next phase of your life so that you can soar, make it happen. If you want to get additional training—perhaps to advance at work or change careers altogether—go get it. In my book *Astronomical Leadership*, I tell my life story of learning how to soar. I also introduce my Input-Process-Output strategy planning session that uses a five-step approach, supplemented by my FRESH WILL methodology, to help you develop a life strategy that will make your goals and dreams an achievable reality. This can then be continued through one-on-one individual coaching sessions that provide the ongoing knowledge you need to make better decisions, sharpen your skills, gain insights into personal and professional growth, and acquire a roadmap to excellence.

If you cannot afford such specialized training or coaching, don't let that deter you. Utilize free library resources or the internet. Information is everywhere. Just determine that you want to soar and will do whatever it takes to do so. You are more than worth it!

Sadly, we don't have to work hard to experience drag and weight in our lives, but finding speed and lift requires more intention. Honestly, this process is not easy, but I can give you hope. There is nothing like soaring. When I began to soar in my career and personal life, my perspective changed tremendously. When you soar in an airplane, the ground and everything on it looks so tiny. When I see mountains through my airplane window, even they look smaller than when I am driving in my car. I want you to have this perspective, too—when even your biggest challenges, including your past failures and hurts, are diminished to where you know you can overcome them.

One more thing. There are far more birds flying close to the ground than there are soaring high in the skies. There are many more airplanes on the ground at the airport than you see in the sky at any given moment. Most of the people around you, even family members, may not be interested in soaring, but don't take that as a message that you should give up on soaring yourself. Be prepared, if necessary, to soar on your own, even without their help.

Pierce grew up in a home where his father and mother were business owners, but Pierce wanted to be a scientist. He had to make a choice: go down the expected path to a traditional job or go after the unexpected and chase his passion. He chose science, knowing he had to go it alone because, even though he had supportive parents, they didn't see how they could specifically help him as entrepreneurs with no knowledge of science. He acquired scholarships, found internships, earned fellowships, and became a biology major working on a master's degree specializing in cancer biology research.

He lifted himself above it all. He soared. I watched Pierce grow up. He was a unique kid. He could've stayed in the average and ordinary, but he chose the path to his passion. It was tough at times, but he did it.

Ashley had five sisters, and they all lived with her grandmother in a very small house. When I moved from Alabama to Arizona after leaving NASA, she moved here with me and my family as an 18-year-old girl. She agreed to come and take care of our son, Jelonni, in return for her going to the University of Arizona to pursue a degree in engineering management. It was an ideal arrangement since both my husband Lonnie and I had full-time jobs, and it was important to us that Jelonni be taken care of by someone who was just like family. Ashley was an itty-bitty thing, weighing no more than a buck ten at best, but even as Jelonni got bigger she held her own with him. Ashley was like a sister to our son, and she was invaluable to us.

She went on to get her degree, get married, and start her own family. She has soared beyond what she could ever imagine.

Sometimes it takes courage to step out and be fearless, confident not in what you see right now, but in what is possible. But you can have that different life. You are meant to soar!

Success Strategy #2

Dreams Point to Purpose

President John F. Kennedy offered a challenge to NASA scientists, technicians, and engineers on May 25, 1961. It was not only daunting. It sounded impossible. He declared, "I believe that this nation should commit itself to achieving the goal, before this decade is out, of landing a man on the moon and returning him safely to the earth."[1]

Kennedy's dream of going to the moon and returning home safely moved the country forward in its thinking about what was possible. There were naysayers. There always are. But NASA and the nation pressed on. When United States astronauts became the first humans to set foot on the moon on July 20, 1969, the morale of the entire country was lifted.

Dr. Werner von Braun, the aerospace engineer and space architect who helped make Kennedy's dream a reality, summed up the achievement this way: "There was dancing in the streets of Huntsville [Alabama] when our first satellite orbited the earth. There was dancing again when the first Americans landed on the moon. There is only one moon. I am afraid we can't offer any such spectaculars like that for some years to come. But I'd like to ask you, don't hang up your dancing slippers."[2]

To soar to your destiny you, too, need to keep your dancing shoes on—and you do that by embracing your dreams. Often, they will point you to a purpose that will ultimately create an incredible reality that you may have never thought possible.

Some belittle the power of dreams. They shouldn't. Without dreams, great things rarely happen. Dreams provide the speed and lift you require to soar.

There are many successful stories of dreams that point to purpose. Three in particular show why discovering and pursuing your dream is essential and beneficial not just to you, but to those around you.

DREAMER #1 – THE BUSINESSPERSON

Joseph was a person who, as a young man, had many dreams of being great, but his family told him to keep his dreams to himself. They did not want to hear about them. He was not the oldest son in his family, and he lived in a culture that strongly prioritized birth order in determining success. So, while his dreams showed him purpose others around him did not understand, he fiercely defended his dreams. As a result, his large family of brothers got so angry with him that they abused Joseph and forced him to move away from his home and to an entirely different country.

Joseph dreamed of being an entrepreneur and a leader within his domain. He also dreamed of being able to help his family—the very family that sent him away—when hard times came. As he embarked on the journey that would lead to the fulfillment of his dreams, Joseph certainly faced more than his fair share of drag and weight. After the emotional and physical abuse caused by his brothers, he was eventually wrongfully accused by his employer and even cast into prison. Joseph had every reason to give up on his dreams, but he had an amazing attitude. He maintained his composure. He didn't give up. He persevered.

Ultimately, he was released from incarceration and placed into a high position of authority. He had to work his way up to the top through rigorous training and discipline, but he made it—exactly like his dreams said he would.

Later, hard times did come. An economic and ecological crisis forced his family to move from their faraway farm all the way to where Joseph was working and leading. They wouldn't survive otherwise. Incredibly, Joseph was in the position to not only help his family, he *saved* them by securing the provisions they needed until the crisis ended. In the end, he was also reconciled to his family, telling them that while they had intended to harm him, everything worked out for good.

For many like Joseph, purpose is hidden in their childhood dreams. He had dreamed of being a leader since he was a boy. Nothing or no one around him suggested that could happen. But he followed his dream, overcame great adversity along the way, and his story had quite a happy ending.

DREAMER #2 – THE LIFE SKILLS ENGINEER

Sarah was in a corporate management position but felt she didn't want to be there any longer. When I asked her what she really wanted to do, she mentioned interior decorating and shared her dream to help others find the beauty in their homes so that they could enhance their enjoyment of living there.

She continued, telling me how her colleagues often came to her for advice about challenges they were facing on the job or ideas on how they could advance in the organization. As Sarah counseled them, she believed she was helping them creatively make their workplace and their responsibilities more enjoyable by seeing the beauty hidden in their own thinking.

I then asked her, "Have you ever considered the fact that you already are an interior decorator—a decorator of people's minds—a designer of thoughts that people can discover and use to help them move forward in life?"

Her face lit up. Suddenly, Sarah saw the reality of her dreams that not only made a positive impact for herself, but also uniquely addressed a felt need and brought value to others around her at that job.

But that wasn't all. She had an additional dream of working with young ladies who needed a confidence boost in their lives. As we talked, I discovered that Sarah was involved with a local community group on the weekends. Through that group, she took that dream and led a special project where she hosted a gathering of high school girls to teach them social graces, general professional skills, and how to write a winning resumé. She then set up individual sessions with each of the ladies to help them to develop personal three- to five-year visions for their lives, including goals for each one to reach her own personal dream.

Amazingly, Sarah became part of what she had originally envisioned—becoming a life coach to young women and inspiring them to see the beauty hidden in their own thinking. In her case, her purpose was already being realized, but she needed to expand her vision to see her dreams come to full fruition.

DREAMER #3 – THE EMERGING ENTREPRENEUR

Remember Meg? At first, it wasn't easy for her to break free from her parents' limited expectation for her to only be a wife and mother. In fact, she didn't believe in her power to pursue her purpose. Instead, when marriage did not come at a young age like she expected, she took on placeholder jobs. She kept telling herself things like, "When I finally get married..." or, "When I have enough money to go back to school..." or, "When I meet the right connections..."

Meg was waiting for circumstances to be right before she pursued her passions. As a result, she spent six years building a career in a field for which she had no passion. She got up, punched the clock, and worked hard for a company that could replace her in the blink of an eye. Therefore, Meg did not perform her job with ambition or enthusiasm, but only did the minimum required. The work felt hard and grueling. Doing a job you don't believe in is often tiring. Meg became exhausted.

One day, she was indeed replaced without warning. Even though she didn't love her job, it was very painful for her to bid it farewell. It was disheartening to think about how little her efforts meant, with long hours spent putting aside her dreams and aspirations to perform a job for someone who wasn't even going to miss her.

It was then Meg realized she never wanted to be replaceable again. Her fate was her own, and she decided to not give it away so easily. Losing her job became a catalyst for finally realizing her potential and determining to fulfill her own dreams.

DREAMER #4 – THE HELPER

Michelle had wanted to be a nurse ever since she was a little girl. She dreamed about helping people and serving their greatest personal needs. When we talked, she was concerned because she had not reached her goals; therefore, she thought she was not going in the direction of her dreams. "I want to help people live more rewarding lives," Michelle said, a note of quiet desperation in her voice.

She proceeded to tell me she had just finished her degree after several years of schooling. I asked her what she had pursued. "Hospital administration," she replied. "I am now working with patients at the local hospital in the billing department."

Success Strategy Personal Profile: Janessa Gory

Janessa Gory is a 15-year-old sophomore in high school who enjoys a variety of things, including photography as her way of capturing moments and being creative in expressing how she sees the world. She also serves on the student council to represent her school, form her leadership skills, and develop them. Her goals are to be successful in life, continue to be a great leader and represent her family name, and be a good example for her younger sibling, nephew, and two nieces. Janessa says she's already looking into colleges, "waiting for what God is going to do for me and what is coming my way." She feels God is leading her to care for others as a nurse, or perhaps play off her natural knack for redesigning, composing, and creating different forms of art to become an architect.

Janessa also has a dream for working with kids of all ages. She loves to help them grow into who they want to be. This passion started early on. She always liked children and being around them. So, after being encouraged by her mother, Jamella, to look for a way to earn some income, Janessa came up with the idea of starting her own babysitting service. She felt it would be something she'd like to do and would be a fun way to make money to buy things she wanted or needed.

Janessa went to work, advertising on Facebook by creating a page and a profile to launch an online community where she reached out to anyone who needed care for their child. People responded and it kept going. She plans to continue her service until she goes to college. "I bounced off of that idea," Janessa said, "and I am very successful in it." Her mother adds, "It is very natural to her. Kids gravitate to her."

In the next chapter, we'll discover how Janessa positioned herself to succeed.

"Then you are doing it!" I told her. "You *are* living your dream; it just looks different than what you expected." She looked at me incredulously. "Don't you see? You are a nurse after all. You're helping sick patients and their families by making it better for them in the billing department." I then encouraged her to show compassion for them right there, as though she were a medical nurse, and serve them as fully as she could in her role as an administrator.

After a few more minutes, it sunk in. "You're right!" Michelle said, chuckling. "Thank you! I love the fact that I am *already* doing what I dreamed."

Michelle discovered how her dreams pointed to her purpose after a change of perspective. All it took was being able to see what she hadn't seen before, and that new outlook gave her renewed joy and direction in her job at the hospital.

Do you feel a longing to help others? First, examine what you are doing at this moment. What aspects serve to assist others or make their lives better or easier? Next, think about other ways you can be a helper outside of work or school. It could be at an area non-profit organization or through your church. Worthy charities are always looking for volunteers. Finally, look at your home life. Are there ways you can be more helpful to your roommate, spouse, or children? That may very well be where you can have the greatest impact of all in fulfilling your dreams as a helper.

DREAMERS NEED HELPERS, TOO

In high school, my sister Yolanda and I used to lay in our beds at night, dreaming about what we wanted to be when we grew up. I asked her, "If you could do anything in life, what would it be?" She said she wanted to travel the world. I then responded, "I want to be on stage." Whether it was as a singer or a musician, I wanted to be a performer—and, more broadly, to be up in front of other people.

Later, I came to understand that my desire to speak in front of people, to guide and influence them, was a leadership trait, and it is something I have certainly fulfilled as an adult. But I didn't get there by myself. Others came along to help provide the speed and lift I needed to soar.

On my first day in Preface at Tuskegee University, I was among about 60 students peppering the seats of the large auditorium. As I looked around, I wondered if I was as wide-eyed as they were. *This is it!* I thought. *I'm here, with all these smart people, and of my own doing.* Professors and leaders within the engineering school were there to greet us, and at the podium was their head, Dr. Jeelani. After a few opening remarks about how Preface was going to work, he said something that put me on alert—and gave me some lift to soar.

"Look at your neighbor," he said, "to your left and to your right, front and back." All of us looked around, heads swiveling. "Only one out of four of you will graduate. The rest of you will not make it in engineering—so you have to make your decision early if this is what you really want to do. Engineering is not for everybody."

His words didn't scare or dissuade me. But they made me realize this was serious, and that I definitely wanted to be among the one out of four who graduated.

Dr. Jeelani took a vested interest in me. He was the one who exhorted me to keep my grades up in the summer program so that I could get a full scholarship. I was really proud and excited about the possibility that my parents wouldn't have to financially help me through college. Another helper I encountered at Tuskegee was a tutor named Blessing. He was one of the smartest guys I ever met. Hailing from Africa, he'd come to the dorm common area dressed in his striped shirt, plaid pants, and stacked platform shoes, snap his fingers, and say with his heavy native accent, "Hellooo! How are you doing?" We'd tell him we needed help. "Yeeees, but eet's a Friday night. You party on a Friday night. Where are you going to partaay?" We'd laugh—and then hit the books. We loved his flamboyant style.

When Preface ended, my grades were strong enough to earn me that full-ride scholarship. It was incredible! All I had to cover was the cost of my books and supplies.

During Preface, we also heard from several speakers who talked to us about goals. That's when I really started setting them for the first time. I charted how many credit hours I needed to get my degree, what classes I wanted to take each semester and why, how many hours per year that was going to cover, and when I wanted to finish. I took to heart what one of the speakers shared: if you set a goal and have an affirmation of that goal, you have a 97 percent probability of reaching it. That amazed me. *All I have to do is write it down, affirm it by repeating it and believing it, and it'll happen?* It was almost too good to be true! But I adapted to that kind of thinking, it worked—and I'm still doing it today.

The encouragement from helpers, and the application of goal setting, gave me all the speed and lift I needed. During my freshman year at Tuskegee, I overcame a few poor grades to maintain my scholarship and ultimately thrived as a student. At the start of my junior year, I was inducted into Eta Kappa Nu, the honor society for the Institute of Electrical and Electronics Engineers. It allowed me to have more interaction with faculty and get invited to key in-house engineering activities. I became a champion and ambassador for the Tuskegee engineering department. As a senior, I was the honor society's vice president. I was also involved with the National Society of Black Engineers. That enabled me to be involved in events such as science fairs and to visit schools to talk to high school students about math and engineering.

Just like that, I started fulfilling that dream to be up in front of other people, influence, and lead. I was beginning to soar!

Whether it's as an entrepreneur, administrator, student, or going to the moon, dream on purpose! Go after your dreams with diligence and steady momentum. Put on those dancing slippers! Your destiny depends on it, for you are a participant in a greater mission that mandates that you add value to the greater good through your best efforts and by maintaining a posture of excellence—which we'll learn more about next.

NOTES

1   President John F. Kennedy, Man on the Moon Speech, Joint Session of Congress, May 25, 1961. http://historicspacecraft.com/quotes.html

2   www.clintburdett.com. Process › Documents: John F. Kennedy Man on the Moon Speech, 1961.

Success Strategy #3

The Posture of Excellence

Have you ever noticed track and field runners right before they begin a race? As they get ready to take their positions on the starting blocks, they may stretch, jump up and down, or even walk back and forth around the area. They may move their heads side-to-side to stretch their necks or extend their arms forward and wind them in circular motions. Perhaps they'll even grab their ankle and pull one of their legs backward to loosen up their hamstring.

These gyrations may seem showy, especially when you add in the magnificent colors these athletes wear. However, it all has a purpose. The exercises and uniforms are designed to give the runner the greatest chance of success and winning the race. The preparation of their muscles and the wind-resistant fabric of their outfits will help them slice through the crowded field of challengers and zoom toward the finish line.

Next, these runners will put their feet in the blocks and torque their bodies into readiness for the starting gun. It's easy to spot the athletes who have excellent trainers because they are more poised and attentive to getting into position than those without proper coaching. In fact, from the time they walk onto the track until the time they leave, their behavior is notable. There is something different about those runners.

They have a posture of excellence.

Now, pause a moment and think about what makes people you admire excellent. Is it their looks, attitude, knowledge, experience, the way they carry themselves, or maybe even their poise and grace? All may point to excellence. The way they behave in tenuous situations and in times of adversity also points to the excellence they possess inside of them.

I equate having a posture of excellence to being in the right place at the right time, except that it's not the result of chance or luck. They have a posture of excellence on purpose. They plan to be there right when they're needed, and they deliver.

THE CORPS (CORE) OF EXCELLENCE

Before starting to promote her editing business, Meg set up a website. She wrote about herself, her history with writing and editing, and her passions. This online presence served as a way to showcase her posture. When she approached authors, she had a place to send them. "If you like what I have to say," her site communicated, "just wait until you see what I've already done!" She backed up her words substantively, with evidence of what she had already accomplished and how she planned to achieve even more. It was her opportunity to present her excellence to others.

I was a member of our high school flag corps. We had to execute each posture when it was signaled to the group. At "parade rest," we could relax our stance a little, moving our legs out to each side so they were a step apart from one another. However, when "attention" was called, we snapped our feet back together so that we were ramrod straight head to toe, except for the bent arms that held the flag. Even as we marched, our feet had to stay in precise position. To be on the flag corps, we had to have a posture of excellence. It was expected. It was noticeable, and excellence was at the core of who we were as members of the team.

And as for being in the right place at the right time—we maintained our posture of excellence when it was time to march in a parade, support the football team from the sidelines, or take the field for the halftime show. We knew each time that our opportunity to perform was nigh and that we had to have the right posture when the show got underway.

Like the runners and the members of my flag corps, some people in our homes, workplaces, and communities are noticeably different in how they present themselves. Without knowing the position they hold or anything about their background, we can see there is something about them that says these people stand out above the crowd—and are able to soar! That's in stark contrast to those who try to give the impression they're more impressive than they really are. People who have a posture of excellence work hard to maintain that posture. If we look close enough, we can notice them practicing certain habits that help them keep their posture. Like a soaring condor whose wings are arched and extended in just the right way, these people are positioned to soar and keep flying high.

PRACTICING GOOD POSTURE

When I was at NASA, I worked with a brilliant engineer from Germany named Bob. He designed rocket engines, and I noticed him reading constantly from three-by-five index cards he carried with him in his shirt pocket whenever there was a lull in the meeting.

"What do you have on those cards?" I asked.

He held a few of them out to me. I saw the small but legible handwriting in ink. "These are formulas for the engines," he said with his decidedly staccato accent. "Designs like this used to be drawn up on napkins or with paper and pencil. I read these again and again so that I know them."

I took a lesson from Bob, got a package of my own 3 x 5 cards, and started carrying them with me. I didn't write equations on mine, though. Instead, whenever I heard a leader say something influential or use a power word or phrase, I immediately wrote it down. Later, I played games with myself using the cards, putting tick marks on each one every time I used what was written on it, or using them like flash cards to retain and memorize a term like "off nominal condition." I created ways to make that content my own, transpose it to increase my knowledge, and improve how I presented myself to others.

I also wrote my dreams and career goals on the cards and read them repeatedly. This process helped define who I was because I was writing what I wanted to accomplish, my destiny, on those cards. I studied my dreams just as Bob studied his equations so that I would be ready for my opportunity to shine. Finally, I even interviewed people to ask them about the kind of experience I would need to achieve my aspirations.

In addition, I made recordings of myself stating my goals, set to a background of jazz music. I would listen to the recordings (back then, on cassette tapes) over and over in the car, even when others were with me. I'm sure they thought I was crazy, but I was determined to reach my goals. I wasn't going to let their criticism or strange looks keep me from doing the preparation that I needed. I was practicing and maintaining my posture of excellence because I wanted to convince myself on every level that I was capable of soaring to great heights.

I reached my initial career goal 20 years *ahead* of when I should've according to the usual timeline of my industry, and all of my peers were at least 20 years older than me. A person with a posture of excellence will outshine their circumstances and sometimes even overachieve on their goals because they do the following:

- Focus on what will develop a pattern to result in a favorable outcome.
- Direct their thoughts and body toward distinction and quality.
- Allow their experiences to shape their behavior toward others and their surroundings.
- Point their self-image away from failure and toward success.
- Know they possess unlimited potential and are highly skilled.

You are made to live and walk in a posture of excellence! Therefore, document your vision and plan your day, week, month, and year in alignment with it. This gives you the greatest opportunity to move in that direction. Even in my high school flag corps, we trained for hours in order to perform with precision. Bob trained his mind to do difficult computations. I educated and drilled myself to reach my goals. So can you!

THE POSTURE OF A DIGNITARY

I'll never forget the day I saw President George W. Bush in person. It was at the memorial service for the crew who lost their lives in the Space Shuttle Columbia accident in 2003. I was still reeling from the disaster as NASA's Director of Safety and Mission Assurance, and he and the First Lady walked right by me on their way to the podium.

I was struck by their majestic demeanor, poised and prepared, exactly what you'd want your leaders to portray, as he readied himself to speak on that poignant, bittersweet day under a sun-splashed sky. "The final days of their own lives were spent looking down on this earth," President Bush said of the crew near the close of his remarks. "And now, on every continent, in every land they could see, the names of these astronauts are known and remembered."

Whenever I see a world leader like a U.S. president or other dignitaries, not one of them is looking at his or her shoes when they walk to the podium. Instead, they look straight ahead, confident and secure, or they will look at someone straight in the eyes when giving them a firm handshake. These people operate in the knowledge that they have vast resources at their disposal to do what they need to do.

Now, close your eyes and imagine yourself being fully in charge of your future. If you had any resource available to you so that you could be given whatever you need to complete your designed assignment, what would you do?

You are an ambassador with a mission—to your city, state, or nation—purposed to make a difference in the lives of others. Believe that you were perfectly designed to fulfill this mission, and that you have the confidence to know what is expected of you. And, just as it is with any dignitary, know that you *are* in charge of soaring to your destiny.

Therefore, maintain your focus and avoid the temptation of lures and distractions that can cause you to lose your posture and mission as a dignitary. That doesn't mean that you shouldn't relax and enjoy life, but beware of anything—from social media to television to extra activities, or even your friends—that captures your attention too frequently or inappropriately. When you yield toward something too much, it can become frivolous and a hindrance to moving forward to fulfill your mission. After all, it's your confidence in your mission and your ability to achieve it that secures your destiny.

WHAT IS A MISSION?

The word "mission" is used a variety of ways. When people say they are "on a mission," they might mean they are determined to get something done. When they say they "conducted a mission,"

> ## Success Strategy Personal Profile: Janessa Gory
>
> Teenager Janessa Gory has launched a successful babysitting service that is creating income for her until she completes high school and goes off to college, perhaps in pursuit of a nursing or architectural design degree as well as to study photography.
>
> She believes she has developed a posture of excellence by reaching out to people who have similar interests to her own. "Whatever I learn from a mentor or a friend or a sibling, I write it all down and take out things that could really help me. I'm always prepared, and I adjust myself for any change that is needed to be made."
>
> Janessa has learned how being teachable and flexible has which positioned her to succeed. She encourages young people in middle school or high school to pay attention to those who are good examples, stay in school and get good grades, strive to be a good example to others (especially younger family members), and to be a good child for their family. She also believes that when you are presented with a challenge and need to create a way to give yourself an opportunity to provide things for yourself, you should come up with a solution. That's what she did with her babysitting service. "Instead of being overwhelmed by it, setting it aside, or getting someone else to take care of it, take care of it yourself."
>
> In the next chapter, you'll find out how Janessa has been able to do what she had never done before.

they could be referring to a military effort or a space flight. When someone says they "do mission work," they probably mean that they travel to different countries to help out needy people. All of these have the same focus: a certain, narrow result that defines what your life is all about.

Missions have five distinct characteristics.

1. Missions seem impossible. That doesn't sound very

encouraging, but the truth is, missions are impossible by every reasonable standard because they are generally endeavors that haven't been done before. But that doesn't mean they can't be done.

The Mission Impossible TV series first aired from 1966-1973 and then again in the late 1980s. You are likely more familiar, though, with the movie franchise starring Tom Cruise that includes six blockbuster motion pictures and more in the works. People have been drawn to the Mission Impossible series for over five decades because they want to experience the highs and lows and the twists and turns that are inevitable during the journey to accomplishing an impossible mission. With each installment, they wonder whether Ethan Hunt will overcome the dastardly foe. The obstacles seem insurmountable, yet he always prevails.

The impossible was possible after all—and if we took that same mindset, more of us would be pursuing our mission instead of avoiding it because it seems too daunting to achieve. You already have all you need inside of you to complete your mission with flawless execution.

2. **Missions are time bound.**

   Although missions may seem impossible to accomplish, the stakes are made even more dramatic because the right resources must be available at a certain time to accomplish them. When entrepreneur Richard Branson set out to cross the Pacific Ocean in a hot air balloon, his first attempt failed. His team waited for the perfect weather conditions. The wind direction was in their favor. The night sky was clear with no clouds in sight. However, on the night of the launch, pieces of the balloon began to peel away. The launch was canceled. Although Branson and his team later completed the mission successfully, the first attempt was lost because the balloon manufacturer delivered a faulty product, causing the initial mission attempt to fail.

3. **Missions are time consuming.** Saying that missions consume time is different from saying that they are time bound, in that we should expect that a mission will take more than a day or two to fulfill. It is not a quick endeavor. School children are taught that astronauts landed on the moon, but they usually don't realize that it took three entire days just to make it from the earth to lunar orbit. The term moonshot is used to describe a lofty goal, but it may also be used by some to misconstrue that getting to the moon was a quick process. It wasn't, and neither is any other mission.

4. **Missions are big.** Missions are large, sometimes gigantic operations that require the right people and the right resources at the right time. The focus of NASA's Apollo program was to get men to the moon. Through a series of missions, it did just that, but these missions were massive. The United States government invested 24 billion dollars in the effort. At one time, the Apollo program employed 400 thousand people and worked with more than 20 thousand other organizations.

5. **Missions are for everyone**
    Whatever your position—math teacher, doctor, nurse, business owner, engineer, writer—you have a role in at least one mission. Often, people have the false belief that their contributions don't mean much, but everyone's contributions are essential to the achievement of a mission. We are all part of something big, and we were created for the times in which we live.

The space program was part of the environment where I grew up. Everyone there was part of something big and took pride in working at the very center of our nation's space mission. Yet as a child, I had no idea that someday I was also going to be part of that mission. But I was, working at NASA for over two decades as an engineer and ultimately serving as Director of Safety and Mission Assurance at the Marshall Space Flight Center. I was the first African American woman to hold that title—a later beneficiary of the courageous women of the motion picture *Hidden Figures* and their missions.

Each one of you possess five things that shapes your mission and secures your posture of excellence.

- A purpose to live for.
- People to live with.
- Principles to live by.
- A profession to live out.
- Power to live on.

These place you in a position of influence as an ambassador to make a difference as you utilize your gifts, talents, education, and abilities. Your mission mandates you to add value to the greater good through your best efforts.

On a sheet of paper, describe what you are doing in your life right now. Write down what is going well. Write down what areas, inside of your control, you see as opportunities to get better. Make note of what is holding you back, and then document the gaps that exist in reaching your desired goal. End by writing down the steps you can take to get to where you want to go. This may require some research. Talking to others who are successful in the area you want to pursue is a great place to start.

In order to understand and fully grasp what you were purposed to be, you must first understand what drives your life and in what (or in whom) you place the most value. The list that you just created will provide this information and allow you to envision where you would like to see yourself five or even 10 years from now.

As you develop a posture of excellence, you can expect to succeed—and start believing in your ability to even do the impossible as you soar to your destiny.

Success Strategy #4

Do What Has Never Been Done Before

M any people were excited about space exploration in the mid-1900s. American and German engineers and scientists agreed they had the ability and technology to do it—but the idea of landing humans on the moon seemed unlikely, even impossible. Astronaut Neil Armstrong estimated the chances of a successful landing were 50-50 at best.

What made the task so hard was the complexity of it all. How could they achieve the thrust necessary to get a manned vehicle into orbit around the earth, much less all the way to the moon? What would it take for the astronauts to actually land the craft travelling at high speeds onto the surface of the moon without crashing? Parachutes or wings wouldn't work in a nearly gravity-free environment with no oxygen in the atmosphere, so the astronauts had to master the output of the thrust. Further complicating a landing was the fact that the craft had to be tilted at just the right angle. Finally, they faced the very real possibility of having to abort the mission at the last moment and return to earth if too much fuel was used.

Failure in any of those challenges—lack of the right atmosphere, the need for precise balancing, limited fuel—could have ended the mission. The astronauts and the NASA staff knew there was no way to guarantee the success of the mission. It was a bit audacious to think they could even pull it off. Yet they went for it anyway. Why? There's was no way they could achieve the goal unless they tried. Whatever the chances, 50-50 or worse, they gave their all to the endeavor.

We know what happened. Incredibly, Apollo 11 became the first spaceflight to land humans on the moon on July 20, 1969. Neil Armstrong ended up being the commander of the flight, and he joined lunar module pilot Buzz Aldrin to actually walk and work on the surface of the moon. Over the next three-and-a-half years, five more manned flights took place before the Apollo program ended. Later, the Space Shuttle program that I became a part of continued the legacy of placing humans into space, always at great risk and sometimes at great cost. Many brave astronauts lost their lives in the process. But we kept trying to do what had never been done before.

Isn't it appropriate, then, that the first lunar module to reach the moon was called the "Eagle?" It's so representative of the idea of soaring to your destiny.

FACING THE POSSIBILITY OF FAILURE

As you pursue your mission on the way to fulfilling your destiny, failure in the short term is always a possibility. But that should never stop you from going after your goals.

We all know the tale of "The Little Engine That Could." There are several versions of the story, and in all of them, a long train must be pulled over a high mountain after its engine breaks down. Larger engines are asked to pull the train, but they refuse. The request is then sent to a small engine, who agrees to try. In one account, that little engine admits she has never been over the mountain. She insists her job is only to move around the other trains in the train yard. Yet the little train engine overcomes her reluctance and diminutive size to accomplish something big, pulling the train over the mountain while repeating its motto, "I think I can!"

Perhaps you've been dutiful in your work, doing the tasks that someone else says you are equipped to do, but you have never left the train yard to accomplish something big. That's where I was for a while, back when I was a well-mannered student who accepted everyone's claim that I was average. I stayed in my comfort zone. I didn't try. But when I finally did choose to break free and go after my goals, I started climbing the mountain. I began to say, "I think I can," until it grew to, "I know I can," as I found my purpose and began to believe in what was possible!

All along, I had to face the prospect of failure. How did I do it? I had to believe that I had what it took within me to move forward toward my goal to become an engineer. I had to realize that obstacles exist not to be in the way, but to be cast aside and conquered. Just before greatness emerges, some people let go under the pressure simply because they can't see what is just on the other side of the obstacles. I also had to keep my faith and start to see things that weren't as though they were.

It's normal to allow fear of the unknown to keep you from aspiring toward greatness, but fear isn't meant to keep you down or hold you back. Sometimes you must allow your fears to be indicators that you're going in the correct direction. If you've ever played a video game, you may have noticed that, when you're advancing in the plot, scary music or difficult situations arise. The little adrenaline rush that comes with those alarm bells lets you know progress is coming and the plot is progressing.

When she was faced with the loss of her job, Meg was afraid to

> ## Success Strategy Personal Profile: Janessa Gory
>
> Fifteen-year-old high school sophomore Janessa Gory drew from her dream and passion to work with kids to launch a babysitting service on Facebook that provides extra income for her to use and enjoy until she is ready to go to college. Few young people her age have done what she has in such a short amount of time, but Janessa credits her mother, Jamella, for setting her up to be able to achieve what she never has before.
>
> "My mom always told me to think outside of the box and to set yourself apart from others," she said. Janessa puts those concepts into practice in her babysitting service as soon as she meets the parents and child. "I get all my information from the parents that I need for the child and emergency contacts. Then I automatically put my attention on the child. I make sure they are comfortable with me. Before the parents leave, they are already warming up to me. I love to make that automatic connection."
>
> Janessa also does the little, extra things that set her apart. She'll have rewards for the children for good behavior or performance, and she'll wipe down counters or put away dishes to help the parents. "I don't like to be just average. I like to be better than that, at a higher level. I think if you always work hard at what you are doing and go above and beyond, you'll get really far."
>
> In the final chapter, we'll see how Janessa's destiny is emerging, and hear more from her mother, Jamella, about pursuing your destiny.

stand on her own and not rely on someone else's success to support her. She needed to pay for basics like food, transportation, insurance, and her home. Rather than letting fear paralyze her or put her back on the wrong path, Meg used those needs to fuel her success. If she didn't achieve her goals, like completing her book or getting hired by authors, she wouldn't be able to pay for her necessities.

The possibility of failure became a compelling motivation to move in the right direction—and she accepted the truth that she could do what she'd never done before.

The same is true of you. You are destined to reach peak performance in all you do. You may not be able to see it just yet, but your success is not only possible, but probable. You have way more than a 50-50 chance! Believe in yourself, and don't let fear of failure hold you back. Be the little engine!

DISS THE DISSUADERS

Some will try to dissuade you from trying for your goals or pursuing your mission. There are even those who, for whatever reason, won't want you to take flight and soar. They will say you are being "unrealistic" or "unwise," that what you want to do is "unheard of," or even tell you that you shouldn't venture into the "unknown" because it's too risky or even illogical.

Refuse these "un-" statements and snub those who seek to discourage or even oppose you. History is replete with those who have not let anything or anyone stop them from believing in the possible and achieving their destiny.

By the time Mahatma Gandhi was born in 1869, the British had been ruling some part of India for over 100 years. British rule was simply an undeniable way of life. As you can imagine, the British had considerable military force as well. There was no logical reason to believe that anything could change regarding British dominance.

Yet something did change. When Gandhi lived in South Africa, he wanted more rights for the Indians living there. He knew that he could not compete with the ruling British government on military grounds. He had no weapons to counter their military force. So, he decided to protest against the British government using nonviolent tactics. Victory was impossible, right? No. Ultimately, Gandhi negotiated a resolution with the government. Later, he used the same courageous tactics to successfully come against the British to bring independence to India. His most famous quote still rings true: "Be the change that you wish to see in the world."

Another person who refused to be held back was Osceola McCarty. She dropped out of school after sixth grade because she needed to care for her ailing aunt, and she never returned. Instead, she made what money she could by washing other people's clothes. Even with her meager income, McCarty managed to save $150,000. When bank officials realized she was amassing a nice sum, they talked to her about what she wanted to do with it. She decided she wanted to help students at her local university.

Her amazing story—from domestic worker to philanthropist—inspired others to donate as well. By 2013, the endowment started in her name had grown to $700,000. Many students have benefited from her gift to the university. Was her achievement looked upon as "unrealistic" or "unheard of?" Sure. But it didn't stop her.

My son, Jelonni, grew up in a family of engineers. I am one, his father is one, and my dad was an engineer, while my dad's father was an electronic technician back in the day doing television and radio repair. Two cousins on my father's side are engineers, as are their kids. Jelonni was surrounded by that influence and the perceived expectation that went with it. But he decided to highlight and expand his creative mind to do something that had never been done before in our family, a completely different path: storyboarding and amination. He has always loved Disney movies. He's watched them over and over, including the credits and the trailers. He has learned the underbelly and the underworkings of animation in movies.

This was all new to us. When I went into engineering, I could talk to my father or any other number of extended family about it, and

Jelonni doesn't have that. But it hasn't dampened his passion for animation or his desire to pursue it. I sat down with him one day and asked him to tell me more about storyboarding in animation. It was fascinating. I then asked him to tell me, "Why animation?" and "Why you?"

In response to the first question, my son said he wanted to do it because he wanted to offer people a way to escape. So many people, he said, are caught up in doing what they do every day, they never get a chance to get out of themselves and their box. I could easily imagine how he'd been looking at all the engineers around him doing our thing and noticed how hard is was for us to get out of our minds for a while. He told me how he wants to use his gifts to allow others to transport themselves into the middle of a story or a scene and be part of something that could take them to a different level of thinking—one where joy, excitement, adventure, and fun are unleashed. Then, Jelonni said, people could return to their everyday lives and responsibilities with more enthusiasm.

That defined his "why." Then we talked a bit about my "why," which is to help people soar above where they are. As we shared, we discovered that my thought processes are more technical, his more artsy, but both of us come together with our own creativity and ingenuity to help others in different ways.

As far as "Why you?" was concerned, Jelonni said he'd bring something that has never been seen before to storyboarding and animation through bringing out his vision and insight for each project he works on, as well as innovate by taking something that someone else has done and leapfroging it to a higher level.

Jelonni had his share of dissauders, those in school and elsewhere who wanted him to be like us or not be what he wanted to be. We all do. During a time when he was most bothered by these dissauders, he took me aside and said he needed my support. He wanted his dad to be proud of him and see what he wanted. He wanted to be supported in what he loved and had a passion to do. We both felt like we were giving him that support, but he needed more. He needed encouragement to be free to feel one way or the other about what everyone else was saying, confident to express his feelings knowing that his family was behind him.

In the end, my son was able to stand up for himself—and he began to take flight.

Success Strategy #5

Destiny Will Emerge

A s you soar, follow your dreams, posture yourself in excellence, and do what has never been done before, your destiny will emerge.

When my son Jelonni told me his "why" for his interest in storyboarding and animation, it was an "aha" moment for both of us. He knew it, and I knew it. He had one cousin who criticized him for watching Disney movies so much, thinking it was inappropriate for a young man to be watching so many cartoons. But his cousin didn't realize that Jelonni wasn't watching the movie as a child would, but as a young adult seeing animation as a profession. Jelonni saw scenes, transitions, and the heroes, villains, and back stories: everything associated with the film.

Jelonni is becoming somewhat of a genius in film history. He is buying books to learn more, and he is asking people what he does well, doesn't do well, and what he needs to work on. Jelonni has even done a GAP Analysis for himself, a tried and true tool to determine what steps need to be taken in order to move from one's current state to its desired, future state. It usually consists of 1) listing characteristic factors (such as competencies and performance levels) of the present situation or "what is," 2) listing factors needed to achieve future objectives or "what should be," and then 3) highlighting the gaps that exist between the two that need to be filled. Jelonni has researched what he needs to do to excel and propel his career forward by filling in the gaps he has identified through that analysis.

As of the writing of this book, my son is 21 years old and a junior at Grand Canyon University. He has discovered that others such as the government and various organizations use animation in addition to the film industry. He is planning to pursue a specific master's degree that will prepare him for employment with those entities.

Jelonni's destiny has begun to emerge. He is excited because he is having conversations with teachers and going to conferences and creative networks where they can share skills and have breakout sessions together. There is clarity in his purpose, and he has talked to some of the best creators and minds in the storyboarding and animation industry. And guess what? I'm excited for him, too.

Je're is another living example of how destiny can emerge. She was a really good student in high school and went off to college to major in engineering. But she found the classes to be different and harder than what she experienced in high school. It was also overwhelming to her being at such a big university. Before long, she left school and returned home, but she wasn't dejected. She was proactive and worked several odd jobs before ending up at a company specializing in inventory for retailers. She travelled to stores throughout her city and surrounding communities, establishing such an excellent reputation that she became a supervisor overseeing a team of people. Je're found the job to be satisfying, and she thought she was successful because she was a supervisor.

Then I had a conversation with her. We agreed that she would never get the benefits of a full-time employee such as a 401(k).

Finally, she didn't have a plan of action for later on in life. I told her, "You need to get a real job."

She looked at me, surprised. "I have a job," she replied, but she also saw something else: potential. As she started applying for other jobs, I encouraged Je're to visualize in her mind what she wanted to do and what kind of job she wanted to have. I directed her to write a letter to herself stating the goals for the type of job she desired.

Guess what happened? She ended up getting a job at a major U.S. defense contractor in security—and she loved it! She's had two or

Success Strategy Personal Profile: Janessa Gory

As you've read about 15-year-old babysitting entrepreneur Janessa Gory, it's clear that she soars to her destiny and has a vision for the future and who see is becoming. She understands that there are steps along the way where she has to soar higher. If the norm is at a certain level, I believe Janessa says, "I see the norm. That is no problem for me. I am going to put extra effort at a higher level, and that will help create the opportunity for me to be able to soar to be the person I am purposed to be."

Janessa's mother, Jamella, is proud of her daughter, and has worked hard to provide the wisdom Janessa needs to soar. "One of the things I teach her is that whatever God gives her that she has a natural knack for, that's what she needs to operate in. He has given her talents and gifts for a reason."

Jamella advises young people in middle school or high school to find that *something* that they do naturally, or that sets them above, and try to go in that direction to see their destiny emerge. "You are still finding yourself and exploring. Stay on the path and stay close to what you know and what your parents have trained you up to be," she said. "Then just continue to pursue the things you know God has put in your heart. Start writing them down so they will make sense to you as you go along."

three promotions since along with merit pay increases to match. Je're was doing something that she never thought she could do, something that had never been done by her before, and she soared! Now she has a 401(k). She is saving for her retirement. She is able to do mighty things! In addition, Je're returned to school to finish her degree.

Je're is continuing to learn to soar in the areas of dominion that she has been given. She is a leader. She has people working for her. She is a respected professional trusted to travel all over the United States on the company's behalf. She can see her destiny emerging right in front of her.

Je're has chosen to stay steady on the course to soar high, but it required her to trust in herself and in the process that I gave her to map out her future and set and pursue her goals. That trust has given Je're the ability to put her all into everything she does and *expect* the best from her situation.

I discovered an amazing story about trust when I traveled to Niagara Falls with my family to celebrate my mother's birthday. The drive from New York to our hotel in Canada was absolutely beautiful, and the hotel itself had a view of the falls from our room. Every night we were captivated by how the falls created and rep-resented majesty. They commanded our respect, while at the same time granting a sense of peace and tranquility as we gazed into the water falling over the rock formations. They seemed to be in perfect harmony with their environment.

Of course, Niagara Falls are a popular honeymoon destination, with an estimated 50,000 couples going there every year. Another interesting fact about the falls is that many notable people have attempted to go down the falls. The very first was a 63-year-old woman who, along with her cat, successfully descended the falls in a barrel. Yet Niagara Falls is perhaps just as popular to other daredevils: tightrope walkers who want to walk across the roaring waters. Many people have attempted the feat over the decades, and some were even successful (though I'm not suggesting that anyone try it themselves; the technical term for tightrope walking is "funambulism," but it sounds anything but fun to me). I can only imagine the preparation and practice required to achieve the venture.

While on a tour there, I read the story of one woman who had watched a tightrope walker succeed in crossing the falls several times and finally had a chance to meet him. "I know who you are," she told him. "You are the tightrope walker."

"Yes," he replied. "How did you know?"

"I have seen you walking over the tightrope and have been happy about your success," she responded.

He smiled. "I am going over again next week. You should come to view the exposition."

The woman called all of her friends and told them about her special invitation, and many of them agreed to attend because it was such an amazing thing to see.

At the event, she went up to the tightrope walker. "I am here. Thank you for inviting me to the event."

Then he asked her a question she didn't expect. "Do you have faith that I will be successful in going over the falls today?"

Without hesitation, she said, "Absolutely!"

He then asked her the same question a second time. She responded, "Yes. I have seen you do it before."

Finally, he said a third time, "Do you believe that I will make it this time?"

She laughed. "Yes, sir. I am confident that you will make it. In fact, I am so sure, I invited all of my friends to see you. They are here to cheer you on."

"If you have faith that I will make it, then," he replied, "how well do you trust me?"

"I trust you completely." It was then that she noticed for the first time that the tightrope walker had a wheelbarrow with him. "What is that for?" she asked.

"That is for me to take over to the other side." Then he looked at her and said, "If you really do trust me, then get in."

You'll recall how Meg had resigned herself for a few years to just working: making an income, getting the bills paid, and going to her job every day. She was successful, but she wasn't fulfilled. Meg wanted to tell stories. She wanted to work with the written word and teach people how to write their best books. Even before dedicating herself to the craft, Meg had a passion for it. She spent her free time breaking down movie and television series plots. She read all the time. She even wrote creatively when she was off the clock! Though exhausted and drained, Meg made time to do what she loved. It was important to her, but she hadn't made it her priority. However, all it took was a little kick in the pants, the loss of her job, to convince her it was time to make the change. She realized she needed to trust in herself and focus on pursuing the thing she loved.

Remember, your destiny will emerge when you have faith to believe in your dreams, get in, and go along for the ride.

Are you ready?

IT'S ALL UP TO YOU!

At the beginning of this book, I asked who you saw in the mirror—and now that you've finished the book, it is my hope that you truly *do* see the real you, the one purposed to be great.

All things are possible if you believe. Will it be fun every day? Probably not. Life has a way of using pressure, challenges, and detours to stretch your creative thinking and cause growth.

Soar to Your Destiny has equipped you with four success strategies on how to win as a person whose attitude rises above all your surroundings. Now it's all up to you. What will you do with what you've discovered?

Aim high. Take flight. Soar!

As a speaker, coach, or trainer, Dr. Amanda H. Goodson will inspire and motivate you with her goal-setting and goal-getting expertise as she pours into you from her unique experiences as a groundbreaking aerospace engineer at NASA, an innovative director at a major engineering company, and encouraging independent certified John Maxwell leadership coach, teacher, and speaker.

She is also author of over 19 books including How to Unlock Your Full Potential: 11 Keys to Leader Success and Authority of a Leader. Amanda is also pastor at Trinity Temple CME Church, and she lives and serves with her family in Tucson, AZ.

To contact Amanda for speaking, coaching,or training, visit:

www.amandagoodson.com

www.ingramcontent.com/pod-product-compliance
Lightning Source LLC
Chambersburg PA
CBHW032018190326
41520CB00007B/531